Knitgrrl Cowls & Scarves

Knitgrrl Cowls & Scarves

ISBN 13 (print): 978-1-937513-89-4

First edition

Published by http://www.cooperativepress.com

Patterns, charts ©2018 Shannon Okey

Photos ©2018 Shannon Okey except pages 22, 44, 47 (Amber Patrick) and pages 10, 14, 17, 26, 36, 51 (Jenn Kidd).

Models: Grace Kontur, Jennifer Davis, Alison Taylor, Kate Snow, Jenn Kidd, Breaya Wilson, Danielle Marx, Shametra Rozzel, Natalia Uribe Wilson

Technical Editor: Andi Smith

Book layout: Shannon Okey and Kim Saar with special thanks to Emily Kuhn for cover help.

Every effort has been made to ensure that all the information in this book is accurate at the time of publication; however, Cooperative Press neither endorses nor guarantees the content of external links referenced in this book.

If you have questions or comments about this book, or need information about licensing, custom editions, special sales, or academic/corporate purchases, please contact Cooperative Press: info@cooperativepress.com or 10252 Berea Rd, Cleveland, Ohio 44102 USA

No part of this book may be reproduced in any form, except brief excerpts for the purpose of review, without prior written permission of the publisher. Thank you for respecting our copyright.

Knitgrrl Cowls & Scarves

Cooperative Press
Cleveland, Ohio

Patterns

Ardal, 6

Asher, 10

Bramley, 14

Brinjal, 18

Casta, 22

Cline, 26

Hermes 3000, 30

Manicorn, 34

Miso, 36

Operetta, 40

Perun, 44

Sarilda, 48

Shadowtime, 52

Intro

This project was overambitious from the very beginning. I looked at my (considerable) yarn stash and declared a problem with the sheer amount. So naturally, I called my tech editor Andi Smith with a ridiculous idea: why not release a pattern a week for a year, and run a Patreon to help fund it?

Andi is more than just my friend and tech editor. She is my co-conspirator, collaborator, enabler, right hand, left brain, and heart. We are teaching road trip road warriors, fiber show booth buddies, sounding boards, middle of the night text messagers and more. Without Andi's skills, this project would never have happened. She takes my gigantic, wild ideas and figures out how to make them reality, and she encourages me along the way without actually making me feel as if perhaps I should tone it down a bit. This book is part of the result!

You can find all the single patterns from this project on Ravelry:

- https://www.ravelry.com/patterns/sources/knitgrrl-patreon

I plan to continue the Patreon after the initial 52 pattern releases:

- https://www.patreon.com/knitgrrl

I knit Brandywine, but sample knitters are the unsung heroes of the knit design industry, and don't get nearly enough pay or credit for all their hard work! Here's who helped me bring these designs to life. Many of them are also designers. Look for them on Ravelry!

- Jen Coican Hovis: Ardal
- Andi Smith: Manicorn, Sarilda
- Judy Njoku: Asher
- April Fehrman: Bramley
- Jen Riester: Brinjal
- Sarah Jo Burch: Casta
- Meg Roke: Cline, Miso, Operetta
- Alison Taylor: Hermes 3000
- Michelle Kroll: Shadowtime

At the end of the book you'll also find a list of Patreon patrons. Their project support funded sample knitting, photography, tech editing and all the other expenses required to bring this to life. Thank you, everyone!

Ardal

I love cables and I love squishy, super-natural fibers like this Rowan Purelife yarn. The two are combined here in a scarf that looks complex but is actually a fairly simple knit once you get going. A good steam block will widen the scarf significantly but only shorten it a bit so be prepare for it to grow wider and open up the cables!

Required Skills

Knitting cables

Knitting bobbles

Working from charts or pattern words

Size

One size

Finished Measurements

60 x 5.5 inches / 152.5 x 14 cm BEFORE blocking and 58 x 7.5 inches / 147.5 x 19 cm after. This opens up quite a bit!

Materials

Rowan Purelife British Sheep Breeds Chunky (100% wool; 120 yds per 100g skein); color: Natural; 3 skeins

US#10.5 / 6.5mm needles

Cable needle

Yarn needle

Gauge

16 sts and 24 rows = 4 inches / 10 cm in stockinette stitch

Stitches and Techniques

Ardal Stitch pattern:

Row 1: P2, k2, p1, k2, p5, 3 st wrap, p1, 3 st wrap, p5, k2, p1, k2, p2.

Row 2 (and all even rows): Work sts as they appear.

Row 3: P1, 2/1 RCp, p1, 2/1LCp, p5, k3, p1, k3, p5, 2/1 RCp, p1, 2/1 LCp, p1.

Row 5: P1, k2, p1, bobble, p1, k2, p5, 3 st wrap, p1, 3 st wrap, p5, k3, p1, bobble, p1, k2, p1.

Row 7: P1, 2/1 LCp, p1, 2/1 RCp, p4, k2tog, k2, yo, p1, yo, k2, ssk, p4, 2/1 LCp, p1, 21 RCp, p.

Row 9: P2, k2, p1, k2, p4, k2tog, k2, yo, p3, yo, k2, ssk, kp4, k2, p1, k2, p2.

Row 11: P1, 2/1 RCp, p1, 2/1 LCp, p2, k2tog, k2, yo, p5, yo, k2, ssk, p2, 2/1 RCp, p1, 2/1 LCp, p1.

Row 13: P1, k2, p1, bobble, p1, k2, p1, k2tog, k2, yo, p1, k2tog, yo, p1, yo, ssk, p1, yo, k2, ssk, p1, k2, p1, bobble, p1, k2, p1.

Row 15: P1, 2/1 LCp, p1, 2/1 RCp, p1, 3 st wrap, p2, yo, ssk, p1, k2tog, yo, p2, 3 st wrap, p1, 2/1 LCp, p1, 2/1 RCp, p1.

Row 17: P2, k2, p1, k2, p2, k3, p2, k2tog, yo, p1, yo, ssk, p2, k3, p2, k2, p1, k2, p2.

Row 19: P1, 2/1 RCp, p1, 2/1 LCp, p1, 3 st wrap, p2, yo, ssk, p1, k2tog, yo, p2, 3 st wrap, p1, 2/1 RCp, p1, 2/1 LCp, p1.

Row 21: P1, k2, p1, bobble, p1, k2, p1, k3, p2, k2tog, yo, p1, yo, ssk, p2, k3, p1, k2, p1, bobble, p1, k2, p1.

Row 23: P1, 2/1 LCp1, p1, 2/1 RCp, p1, 3 st wrap, p2, yo, ssk, p1, k2tog, yo, p2, 3 st wrap, p1, 2/1 LCp, p1, 2/1 RCp, p1.

Row 25: P2, k2, p1, k2, p2, yo, k2, ssk, p1, k2tog, yo, p1, yo, ssk, p1, k2tog, k2, yo, p2, k2, p1, k2, p2.

Row 27: P1, 2/1 RCp, p1, 2/1 LCp, p2, yo, k2, ssk, p5, k2tog, k2, yo, p2, 2/1 RCp, p1, 2/1 LCp, p1.

Row 29: P1, k2, p1, bobble, p1, k2, p3, yo, k2, ssk, p3, k2tog, k2, yo, p3, k2, p1, bobble, p1, k2, p1.

Row 31: P1, 2/1 LCp, p1, 2/1 RCp, p4, yo, k2, ssk, pk1, k2tog, k2, yo, p4, 2/1 LCp1, p1, 2/1 RCp, p1.

Pattern

Cast on 33 sts.

Foundation Row 1: P2, k2, p1, k2, p5, k3, kp1, k3, p5, k2, p1, k2, p2.

Foundation Row 2: K2, p2, k1, p2, k5, p3, k1, p3, k5, p2, k1, p2, k2.

Work repeats of chart or patternwords, then work Rows 1–6 once. Bind off in pattern.

Finishing

Weave in all ends and block to measurements.

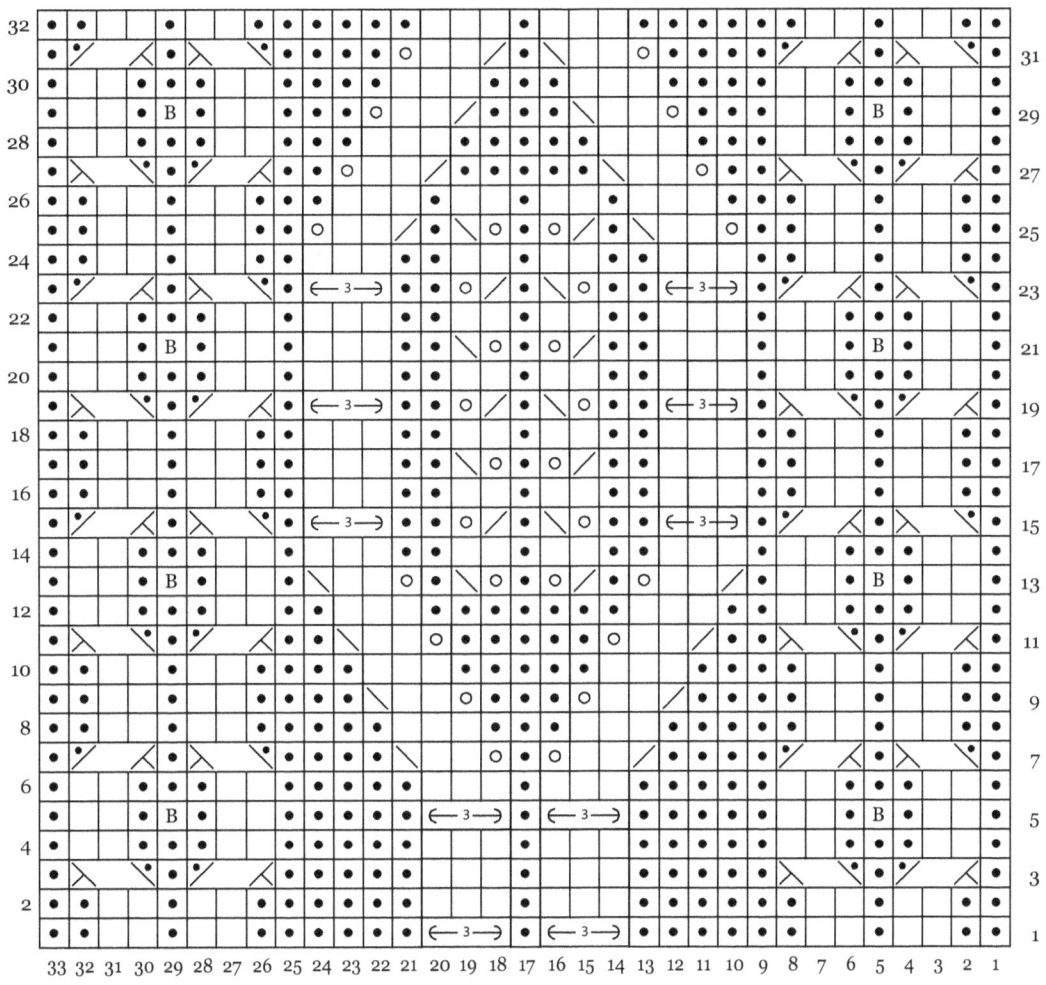

Asher

Looking for a scarf that meets both the "not boring to knit" for the knitter AND the "yes, my significant other or family member will wear this willingly" requirements? Believe me. I've been there. I have revoked handknits from people who do not appreciate the time they took to knit. Asher is knit on a very long needle from side to side which I personally find helpful in eliminating the This Will Never Be Long Enough dread of some scarves.

Required Skills

Required Skills

Basic knitting skills

Working simple stitches from written instructions

Size

One Size

Finished Measurements

Width: 7 inches / 18 cm

Length: 68 inches / 173 cm

Materials

Cascade Yarns Cascade 220 (100% wool; 220 yds / 201m per 100g skein); color: 8914 Granny Smith; 3 skeins

1 32-inch US#7 / 4.5 mm circular needles - or longer

14 stitch markers - optional

Yarn needle

Gauge

18 sts and 26 rows = 4 inches / 10 cm in stockinette stitch

Pattern Notes

This textured scarf is worked lengthwise, hence the need for a very long circular needle. The edges—lengthwise —are worked in garter stitch. The body of the scarf is worked in a repeating seeded chevron pattern.

Stitches and Techniques

Garter Stitch

All rows: Knit.

Seeded Chevron (worked over 22 sts)

Row 1: K1, * p3, [k1, p1] twice, k1, p5, k1, [p1, k1] twice, p3, k1; repeat from * to end.

Row 2: P1, *p1, k3, [p1, k1] twice, p1, k3, p1, [k1, p1] twice, k3, p2; repeat from * to end.

Row 3: K1, *k2, p3, [k1, p1] five times, k1, p3, k3; repeat from * to end.

Row 4: K1, *p3, k3, [p1, k1] four times, p1, k3, p3, k1; repeat from * to end.

Row 5: P1, *p1, k3, p3, [k1, p1] three times, k1, p3, k3, p2; repeat from * to end.

Row 6: K1, *k2, p3, k3, [p1, k1] twice, p1, k3, p3, k3; repeat from * to end.

Row 7: K1, *p3, k3, p3, k1, p1, k1, p3, k3, p3, k1; repeat from * to end.

Row 8: K1, *[p1, k3, p3, k3] twice, p1, k1; repeat from * to end.

Row 9: K1, *p1, k1, p3, k3, p5, k3, p3, k1, p1, k1; repeat from * to end.

Row 10: K1, *p1, k1, p1, [k3, p3] twice, k3, [p1, k1] twice; repeat from * to end.

Row 11: K1, * [p1, k1] twice, p3, k3, p1, k3, p3, [k1, p1] twice, k1; repeat from * to end.

Row 12: K1, * [p1, k1] twice, p1, k3, p5, k3, [p1, k1] three times; repeat from * to end.

Row 13: P1, *[p1, k1] three times, p3, k3, p3, [k1, p1] twice, k1, p2 repeat from * to end.

Row 14: K1, *k2, [p1, k1] twice, [p1, k3]twice, [p1, k1] three times, k2; repeat from * to end.

Pattern

Cast on 309 sts.

Row 1: K1, knit to end of row, placing stitch markers every 22 sts to denote pattern repeats.

Row 2: Knit, slipping markers as you come to them.

Row 3: Work 14 repeats of first row of Seeded Chevron stitch pattern across.

Row 4: Work 14 repeats of second row of Seeded Chevron stitch pattern across

Continue working Rows 3–14 across all sts, then work stitch pattern Rows 1–14 twice.

Rows 45 and 46: Knit.

Bind off.

Finishing

Weave in all ends and steam or wet block to measurements.

Bramley

I'm thoroughly in love with Blue Moon Fiber Arts' Raven Clan colorways. If you view them from afar they almost look alike, but up close the subtle variations really grab you. This yarn was purchased during one of their open houses on a trip to Oregon. Among other wonders I got to witness someone dyeing their hair in an indigo bath out back near the chickens. Amazing!

Required Skills

Basic knitting skills

Decreases

Increases

Working lace from chart or written instructions

Size

One size

Finished Measurements

Width: 15 inches / 38 cm

Length: 64 inches / 162.5 cm

Materials

Blue Moon Fiber Arts Gaea Worsted (100% wool; 305 yds / 279 m per 226g skein); in Ravenscroft or any of the Raven Clan colorways: 2 skeins or 550 yards of chunky weight yarn

US#10.5 / 6.5mm circular or straight needles or size needed to obtain gauge

Yarn needle

Gauge

14 sts and 18 rows = 4 inches / 10 cm square in stitch pattern, after blocking

Pattern Notes

This scarf is worked flat from the bottom up. It features alternating sections of garter stitch pattern and a garter fan lace stitch pattern.

Stitches and Techniques

Garter Fan Lace (worked over 15 sts)

Row 1: K5, p2tog, yo, p1, yo, spp, k5.

Rows 2, 4, 6, 8, 10: P7, k1, p7.

Row 3: K4, p2tog, [p1, yo] twice, p1, spp, k4.

Row 5: K3, p2tog, p2, yo, p1, yo, p2, spp, k3.

Row 7: K2, p2tog, p3, yo, p1, yo, p3, spp, k2.

Row 9: K1, p2tog, p4, yo, p1, yo, p4, spp, k1.

Row 11: P2tog, p5, yo, p1, yo, p5, spp.

Row 12: Purl.

Garter Stitch

All rows: Knit.

Pattern

Cast on 49 sts using long tail cast on or preferred method of cast on.

Work in garter stitch for 14 rows (or 3.5 inches / 9 cm).

Rows 1–12: K2, work across Rows 1–12 of the Garter Fan Lace Chart, repeating the 15-st pattern 3 times across.

Repeat Rows 1–12 two more times (three repeats total).

Work in garter stitch for 14 rows (or 3.5 inches / 9 cm).

Repeat the last 50 rows five more times.

Bind off knit-wise.

Using a yarn needle, weave in all ends.

Finishing

Steam or wet block to measurements. Be careful when wet-blocking this scarf. Garter stitch likes to grow!

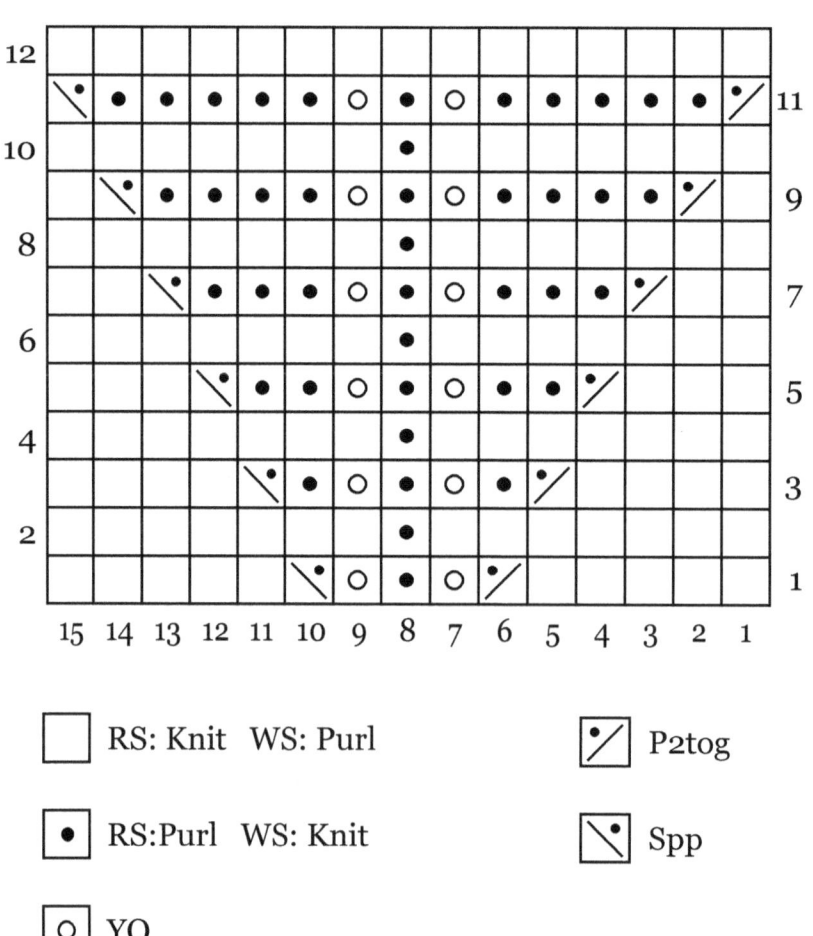

Brinjal

Sometimes you don't NEED yarn but you HAVE to have it, and that was the case with this particular skein, dyed by Megan Ingman of Lichen and Lace, the former owner of Lettuce Knit in Toronto (one of my all-time favorite yarn stores). The pattern name derives from another word for eggplant or aubergine used in South Africa and South Asia.

Required Skills

Knitting in the round

Simple increases/decreases

Bobbles

Following pattern from chart or words

Size

One size

Finished Measurements

Width: 12 inches / 30.5 cm

Length: 6.5 inches / 16.5 cm

Materials

Lichen and Lace 4 ply Worsted (100% Merino; 200 yds per 115g skein); color: Baby Eggplant; 1 skein

US#8 / 5mm circular needles

Stitch marker

Yarn needle

Gauge

16 sts and 24 rows = 4 inches / 10 cm in stockinette stitch

Pattern Notes

It can be difficult to read gauge on this cowl while knitting: if you're happy with the fabric you're knitting and within range of the given gauge, you'll be fine.

Stitches and Techniques

b - bobble: Make bobble thus: (k, p, k, p, k) into next st, turn. Purl 5, turn. K2tog, k3togtbl, pass k2tog stitch over.

Brinjal stitch pattern (worked over 16 sts)

Rnd 1: P1, k1tbl, p1, ssk, k3, yo, k1, yo, k3, k2tog, p1, k1tbl.

Rnd 2 (and all even rnds): Work sts as they appear.

Rnd 3: P1, k1tbl, p1, ssk, k2, yo, k3, yo, k2, k2tog, p1, k1tbl.

Rnd 5: P1, k1tbl, p1, ssk, k1, yo, k5, yo, k1, k2tog, p1, k1tbl.

Rnd 7: P1, k1tbl, p1, ssk, yo, k3, bobble, k3, yo, k2tog, p1, k1tbl.

Rnd 9: P1, k1tbl, p1, ssk, yo, k2, bobble, k1, bobble, k2, yo, k2tog, p1, k1tbl.

Rnd 11: P1, k1tbl, p1, ssk, yo, k7, yo, k2tog, p1, k1tbl.

Rnd 13: K1, yo, k3, k2tog, p1, [ktbl, p1] twice, ssk, k3, yo.

Rnd 15: K2, yo, k2, k2tog, p1, [ktbl, p1] twice, ssk, k2, yo, k1.

Rnd 17: K3, yo, k1, k2tog, p1, [ktbl, p1] twice, ssk, k1, yo, k2.

Rnd 19: Bobble, k3, yo, k2tog, p1, [ktbl, p1] twice, ssk, yo, k3.

Rnd 21: K1, bobble, k2, yo, k2tog, p1, [ktbl, p1] twice, ssk, yo, k2, bobble.

Rnd 23: K4, yo, k2tog, p1, [ktbl, p1] twice, ssk, yo, k3.

Rnd 24: As Rnd 2.

Pattern

Using your favorite stretchy method, cast on 144 sts. Being careful not to twist, join to work in the round, placing a marker to denote the beginning of the round.

Rnd 1: *P1, k1tbl; repeat from * to end of rnd.

Rnds 2 and 3: As Rnd 1.

Rnd 4: Work 9 repeats of Rnd 1 of chart or Brinjal stitch pattern words.

Work Rnds 1–24 of stitch pattern twice. Bind off in pattern.

Finishing

Weave in all ends and block to measurements. Note that this cowl won't block out much larger than it is on the needles thanks to the density of the stitch pattern.

Legend

- ☐ Knit
- ℟ K1tbl
- • Purl
- ○ YO
- ╱ K2tog
- ╲ Ssk
- B Bobble

Casta

"Casta" means "twisted" in Irish, and as this is a cabled pattern knit in Tahki's Tara Tweed, I thought it an appropriate name for this pretty little cowl. This is a fairly quick knit and perfect for those in-between weather days where you don't want to wear a huge scarf to stay warm but need something to ward off the chill. The loftiness of the yarn traps plenty of warm air right where you need it.

Required Skills

Required Skills

Knitting in the round

Simple cables

Following directions from words or chart

Size

One size

Finished Measurements

Circumference: 32 inches / 81 cm

Height: 6 inches / 15.25 cm

Materials

Tahki Yarns Tara Tweed (80% Wool, 20% Nylon; 122 yards per 50 gram skein) 2 skeins Cherry Tweed #16

1 32-inch US#8 / 5mm circular needle

Stitch marker

Yarn needle

Gauge

18 sts and 26 rnds = 4 inches / 10 cm in stitch pattern after blocking

Pattern Notes

Casta begins with a ribbed border that will set you up for the cables to come.

Casta Cable pattern

Rnd 1: P1, k2, p4, 2/2 LC, p4, k2, [p4, 2/2 LC] twice, p3.

Rnds 2, 3 & 4: P1, k2, p4, k4, p4, k2, [p4, k4] twice, p3.

Rnd 5: As Rnd 1.

Rnd 6: As Rnd 2.

Rnd 7: P1, k2, p4, k4, p4, k2, p2, work [2/2 RCp, 2/2 LCp] twice, p1.

Rnd 8: P1, k2, p4, k4, p4,k2, p2, k2, p4, k4, p4, k2, p1.

Rnd 9: P1, k2, p4, 2/2 LC, p4, k2, p2, k2, p4, 2/2 LC, p4, k2, p1.

Rnd 10: As Rnd 8.

Rnd 11: P1, [2/2 LCp, 2/2 RCp] twice, p2, k2, p4, k4, p4, k2, p1.

Rnds 12, 14, 15, 16, & 18: P3, [k4, p4] twice, k2, p4, k4, p4, k2, p1.

Rnds 13 & 17: P3, [2/2 LC, p4] twice, k2, p4, 2/2 LC, p4, k2, p1.

Rnd 19: P1, [2/2 RCp, 2/2 LCp] twice, p2, [2/2 LCp, 2/2 RCp] twice, p1.

Rnd 20: As Rnd 2.

Cowl Pattern

Cast on 180 sts.

Being careful not to twist, join to work in the round, adding a stitch marker to denote the beginning of the round.

Ribbed border begins:

Rnd 1: *[P1, k2] twice, [p2, k2] twice, [p1, k2] twice, [p2, k2] 4 times; repeat from * around.

Work Rnd 1 a total of 8 times.

Cabled body begins:

Rnd 9: As Rnd 2 of chart, or Casta Cable pattern.

Work Rnds 3–20 once, then rnds 1–10.

Ribbed border to end cowl:

Work 8 rnds of ribbing as per first ribbed border.

Bind off in pattern.

Finishing

Weave in ends and lightly block (a quick shot of steam was enough to even out the stitches and make the cables pop for this particular yarn; your yarn may vary).

Key

- ☐ Knit
- ⊡ Purl
- ⧖ 2/2 LC
- ⧖ 2/2 LCp
- ⧖ 2/2 RC
- ⧖ 2/2 RCp

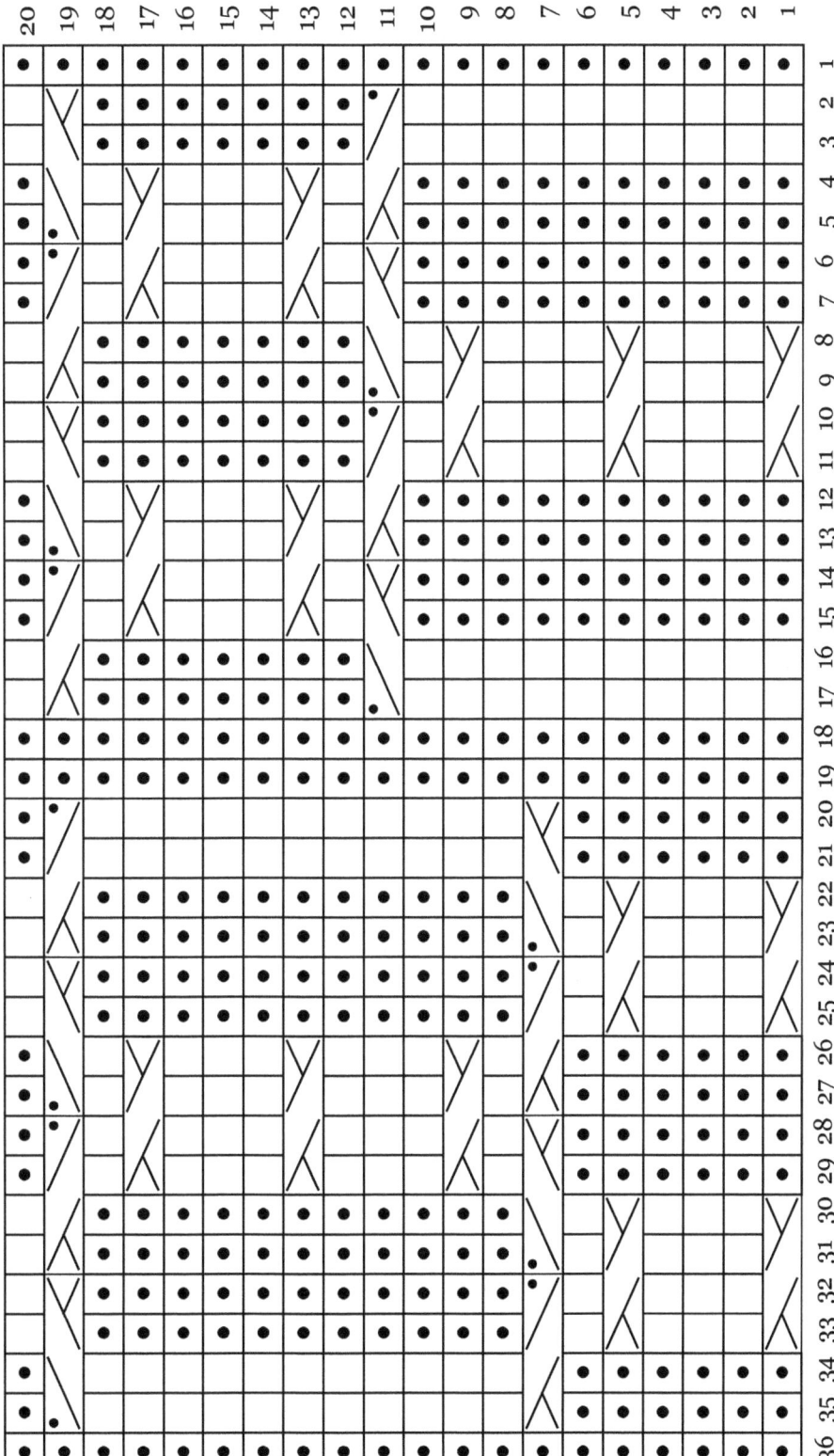

Cline Cowl

Are you a Patsy Cline fan? You can blame my grandmother for getting me into her music. When I look at the triangles in this pattern for too long I get Patsy's song "Triangle" caught in my head. Not the worst earworm in the world, but still... tra la la la, triangle. Simple pattern but big learning opportunity if you're afraid of combining colors: read on for a fun tutorial and some coloring pages so you can experiment.

Required Skills

Basic knitting skills

Knitting in the round

Working from colorwork chart

Working corrugated single ribbing

Size

One size

Finished Measurements

Circumference: 24 inches / 61 cm

Length: 8 inches / 20.5 cm

Materials

Brooklyn Tweed Shelter (100% American wool; 140 yds / 128m per 50g skein); color: 1 skein each in Tartan (MC) and Cinnabar (CC), or 100 yards (in MC) and 75 yards (in CC) of worsted weight yarn

16 inch US#7 / 4.5mm circular needles or size needed to obtain correct gauge

Stitch markers

Yarn needle

Gauge

20 sts and 24 rnds = 4 inches / 10 cm in stockinette stitch colorwork pattern on US#7 /4.5mm needles, or size needed to obtain correct gauge

Pattern Notes

This cowl is worked in the round from the bottom up. The bottom and top edge are worked in a single corrugated rib. The body of the cowl features a repeating triangle colorwork pattern worked in stockinette stitch.

If you wish to knit a larger version by adding additional stitch repeats, you may run out of MC yarn. Consider buying an extra skein, or eliminating the corrugated ribbing.

Stitches and Techniques

Corrugated Single Rib

All Rnds: [K1 in MC, p1 in CC], to end.

Stockinette Stitch

All Rnds: Knit.

Pattern

With MC, using long tail method, cast on 120 sts, and being careful not to twist, join to work in the round.

Place marker to denote beginning of the round.

Rnds 1–4: Work in corrugated single rib.

Rnds 5–6: Knit in MC only.

Work Rounds 1–6 of chart, repeating 6-stitch pattern 20 times around.

Repeat chart a total of 6 times (42 total rounds, 36 rounds of chart)

Rnds 43–44: Knit in MC only.

Rnds 45–48: Work in corrugated single rib.

Bind off in MC only, maintaining single rib pattern as established

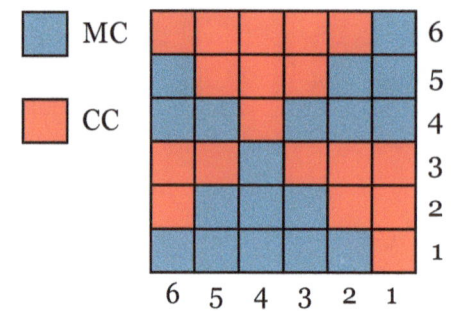

Finishing

Using a tapestry needle, weave in all ends.

Steam or wet block to measurements.

Color me!

Want to test out a color combo before you start knitting? Here are some blank pattern repeats you can color. Use the darker of your chosen colors on the grey squares. Tag pictures of your color masterpieces with #clinecowl on social media so we can see your masterpieces.

Hermes 3000

Why Hermes 3000? After the first sample was knit, the colors reminded me of the keys on my vintage Swiss Hermes 3000 typewriter (see photo). After acquiring that model plus an even older Olympia from a family estate sale I'm honestly getting the collector bug (help!). This cowl is simple to knit but is an excellent way to exercise control over color dominance and how you carry yarn for stranded knitting. It would also be a great stashbusting/scrappy pattern!

Required Skills

Knitting in the round

Working from colorwork chart

Size

One size

Finished Measurements

Circumference: 23 inches / 58 cm

Height: 6.5 inches / 16.5 cm

before blocking

(with 2.5 repeats of chart pattern)

Materials

MC: The Fibre Co. Organik (70% Wool, 15% Baby Alpaca, 15% Silk; 98 yds / 90 m per 50g / 1.76 oz skein); color: Fjord; 2 skeins

CC1: The Fibre Co. Terra (40% Wool, 40% Baby Alpaca, 20% Silk; 196 yds / 179 m per 100g / 3.53 oz skein); color: Mint; 1 skien

CC2: The Fibre Co. Acadia (60% Wool, 20% Silk, 20% Baby Alpaca; 145 yds / 133 m per 50 g / 1.76 oz skein); color: Summersweet; 1 skein

US#8 / 5 mm circular needle

1 stitch marker

Yarn needle

Gauge

24 sts and 32 rounds = 4 inches / 10 cm in pattern stitch

Pattern Notes

Aim for loose floats as you're knitting this. Tight floats are never a good thing but when you're getting three yarns of slightly-different-weight to play together nicely in the body of one fabric they can be disastrous.

A note from the original sample knitter: because there are three different yarns here it is also important to make sure you are paying attention to color dominance / what position each yarn is in as you knit.

It doesn't matter which so long as you're consistent. For a great post on this topic, check out Ysolda Teague's blog here:

https://ysolda.com/blogs/journal/colour-dominance

(shorter: https://bit.ly/2xTe99n)

Cowl width can be adjusted by adding or subtracting multiples of 8 to/from beginning stitch count.

Pattern

With MC, cast on 160 sts, and being careful not to twist, join to work in the round, placing a marker to denote the beginning of the round.

Joining CC2, work 5 rnds of Bottom Edging pattern, then work 2.5 repeats of main colorwork pattern or until you are nearly out of yarn. (If you are doing this as a stashbusting pattern, feel free to keep going!)

Finish cowl by working 5 rnds of Top Edging pattern, then bind off alternating knit and purl stitches for flexibility using MC.

Finishing

Weave in all ends and wet block.

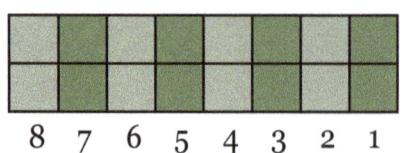

Top Edge

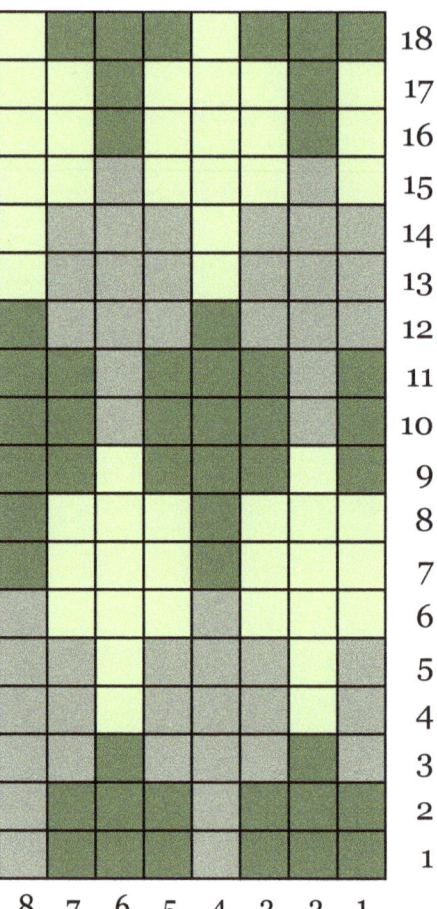

Bottom Edge

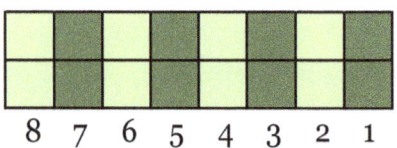

MC   CC1   CC2

Manicorn Cowl

Manicorn is our new studio mascot, aka what happens when you find a bunch of mannequin torsos in the new building and you already have a unicorn mask...

He's full of rainbows so he loves this speckled multicolor MadTosh yarn!

Required Skills
Knitting in the round

Following pattern from words

Simple decreases

Size
One size

Finished Measurements
Circumference: 27 inches / 68.5 cm

Height: 8 inches / 20.25 cm

Materials
Madelinetosh Tosh DK (225 yds / 206 m per 100 g skein); colorway Cosmic Wonder Dust; 1 skein

US#7 / 4.5mm circular needle

Yarn needle

Gauge
20 sts and 26 rounds = 4 inches / 10 cm in pattern stitch.

Pattern
Using long-tail, or your favorite stretchy method, cast on 140 sts. Being careful not to twist, join to work in the round, adding a stitch marker to note the beginning of the round.

Rnds 1–4: *K1, p1; repeat from * to end of rnd.

Rnd 5: *Yo, k2tog; repeat from * to end of round.

Work 44 repeats of Round 5.

Rnds 50–53: Repeats rnds 1–4.

Bind off loosely.

Finishing
Weave in ends. Steam block lightly.

Miso Scarf

Garter stitch doesn't get nearly enough respect. It's versatile, pretty, and shows off many different yarn styles well. Why "Miso"? I'm a giant fan of miso, not just as soup, and am currently learning to ferment it from scratch. Miso seems plain and boring, but it adds a LOT to anything you use it in... just like garter stitch! This would be a great starter project for teaching a new knitter, or for using up scraps of similar yarn.

Required Skills

Basic knitting skills

Working simple stitches from written instructions

Size

One size

Finished Measurements

(before blocking)

Length: 67 inches / 170 cm

Width: 9.5 inches / 24 cm

Materials

Malabrigo Yarn Arroyo (100% merino wool; 335 yds / 306m per 100g skein); color: Borrajas: 2 skeins

US#5 / 3.75 mm straight or circular needles

Yarn needle

Gauge

20 sts and 40 rows = 4 inches / 10 cm in garter stitch (before blocking) or size needed to obtain gauge.

Pattern Notes

This textured scarf is worked flat from the bottom up in garter stitch. There is a repeating stockinette stitch little check pattern. Please note that garter stitch grows exponentially when wet blocked. The finished measurements provided are before blocking. The sample pictured was gently steam blocked to reduce unwanted growth. Even with steam blocking, the sample grew about 12 inches/30.5 cm. Additionally, this scarf pattern was designed to use up two complete skeins of Arroyo yarn. Please keep this in mind when substituting yarn.

Stitches and Techniques

Garter Stitch

All rows: Knit.

Little Check (over 3 stitches)

Rows 1 and 3: Knit

Rows 2 and 4: Purl

Pattern

CO 47 sts.

Rows 1-21: Knit (approximately 2 inches / 5cm ending with a RS row).

Row 22 (WS): K8 [p3, k11] two times, p3, k8.

Row 23: Knit

Repeat Rows 22 and 23 once more.

Rows 26-46: Knit (approximately 2 inches / 5 cm ending with a RS row).

Row 47 (WS): K15, p3, k11, p3, k15.

Row 48: Knit.

Repeat Rows 47 and 48 once more.

Repeat Rows 1-50 twelve times more. (650 rows or 325 garter ridges total)

Knit 21 rows (approximately 2 inches / 5cm ending with a RS row).

Bind off.

Finishing

Weave in all ends.

Gently steam block to measurements.

Operetta Scarf

Sometimes you need a simple knit—for traveling, the movies, or for knitting in a room full of non-knitters who don't know that face you're making means "shut up, I'm counting!" This fits the bill in a most elegant way, and makes the most of one of my favorite yarn skeins. Before it was knit up I had been known to pet the Petworth...

Required Skills

Basic knitting skills

Working simple stitches from written instructions

Size

One size

Finished Measurements

Length: 60.5 inches / 153 cm

Width: 6 inches / 15 cm

Materials

Neighborhood Fiber Co. Yarn Studio Worsted (100% merino wool; 400 yds / 366m per 228g skein); color: Petworth, 1 skein

40+ inch / 101+ cm US#5 / 3.75 mm circular needles, or size needed to obtain gauge

Yarn needle

Gauge

22 sts and 29 rows = 4 inches / 10 cm in rib stitch

Pattern Notes

This textured scarf is worked flat lengthwise in a particular rib stitch pattern. Please note that rib stitch, when worked lengthwise, grows exponentially when wet blocked.

The finished measurements provided are after gentle steam blocking (to reduce unwanted growth).

This scarf pattern was designed to use up one complete skein of Studio Worsted yarn. It takes about 5 grams/ 9 yards of this yarn to bind off. Keep this in mind when substituting yarn.

Stitches and Techniques

Rib Stitch

Row 1: K3 *p1, k4; rep from * to last 3 sts, k3.

Row 2: *P2, k3; rep from * to last 2 sts, p2.

Pattern

CO 332 sts.

Rows 1 (RS): K3 *p1, k4; rep from * to last 3 sts, k3.

Row 2 (WS): *P2, k3; rep from * to last 2 sts, p2.

Repeat rows 1–2 until piece measures 6 inches / 15 cm ending with a WS row, or until 5 grams/ 9 yards of yarn remain.

Bind off loosely in established pattern.

Finishing

Using a tapestry needle, weave in all ends.

Please see Pattern Notes above for stitch-based blocking recommendations.

Perun Cowl

Perun is the Slavic god of thunder and lightning. The "thunder marks" representing Perun found on pottery and house roof beams echo the round shape of this cowl and its openings. What can I say? I read too many mythology books. This cowl was designed for New York Fashion Week February 2017 specifically to complement necklaces by my designer friend Lauren Tatum of bunnypaige.com and it can be worn a very large number of ways, even as a top!

Required Skills
Basic knitting skills
Knitting in the round
Casting off mid-row
Casting on mid-row

Size
One size; easily adjusted

Finished Measurements
Circumference: 41 inches / 104 cm

Height: 21 inches / 53 cm

These measurements are post-blocking and are approximate (taken with "buttonholes" pushed closed, flat on a table—piece will grow when worn/held up vertically)

Materials
Malabrigo Caracol (100% superwash Merino wool; 90 yds / 82m per 150g skein); color: Cirrus Gray; 4 skeins

US#10 32-inch circular needles

Yarn needle

8 removable stitch markers (helpful if one is different color to mark beginning of round)

Gauge
12–14 sts and 16–18 rnds = 4 inches / 10 cm

Please note: this is a thick-thin yarn and gauge is highly variable. As long as your fabric falls within these ranges, you'll be fine.

Pattern Notes
This cowl is worked in the round and 2-row buttonhole openings (bind off on one round, cast back on for the next) are spaced out over multiple buttonhole rounds to create openings that will allow the cowl to be worn in multiple ways (even as a top, if you are so inclined!).

Stitch markers will be the key to your sanity on these rounds but when binding off the stitches, there will always be one stitch left, so you'll cast back on one fewer stitch per opening on the next round to remain at the same total number of stitches in the round.

Pattern

CO 110 sts using long tail cast on or preferred method of cast on. Due to the thick-thin nature of the yarn and its price per skein, I would recommend casting on using two skeins at once so there's as little waste as possible.

Put a slipknot at the end of the two strands and position yarn as if for long tail cast on with a single doubled strand of yarn. When finished casting on the required number of stitches, cut second strand and continue with pattern as written.

Place different colored marker (to distinguish beginning of round marker from those that will be placed later) and join to work in the rnd.

Knit 27 rounds.

Buttonhole round 1:

Bind off 25, PM, knit 10, PM, bind off 10, PM, knit 10, PM, bind off 25, PM, knit 10, PM, bind off 10, PM, knit 10.

Cast on Round 1:

Slipping all markers as you come to them, cast on 24, knit 10, cast on 9, knit 10, cast on 24, knit 10, cast on 9, knit 10.

Remember, you will have a leftover stitch from the bind off on the previous round at the end of each "buttonhole," so your total number of stitches should once again be 110. You will also need to slip the stitch marker at the beginning of each buttonhole to the right side of that leftover stitch before you cast on the new stitches.

Knit 17 rounds and remove all markers except beginning of round marker.

Buttonhole Round 2:

Knit 10, PM, bind off 10, PM, knit 10, PM, bind off 25, PM, knit 10, PM, bind off 10, PM, knit 10, bind off 25.

Cast on round 2:

Slipping all markers as you come to them, knit 10, cast on 9, knit 10, cast on 24, knit 10, cast on 9, knit 10, cast on 24.

Once again you should be at 110 stitches.

Knit 17 rounds and remove all markers except beginning of round marker.

Repeat Buttonhole Round 1.

Repeat Cast On Round 1.

Remove all markers except beginning of round and knit 27 rounds.

Bind off and weave in ends.

Finishing

This particular yarn is a very fluffy thick and thin yarn with a thread plied around it to provide texture.

As such, it is a *beast* to wet block and takes forever to dry. I recommend heavy steam blocking instead.

When I wet blocked the sample, the sheer amount of water soaked up in the yarn itself made for a challenging drying time, and the weight of the water distorted the fabric, which needed to be supported on all sides in order to dry without stretching.

How to Wear It

I've known Shametra since I taught a summer textiles program when she was in high school, and have been fortunate enough to watch her do amazing work at fashion school, and go on to a professional career in fashion and textiles. She's my fave. She's also a fantastic model! Here are some photos from the shoot showing you all the different ways we draped it. Arm in one hole. Arms in two holes. On the neck. Off the shoulder. You get the idea: it's very flexible!

Necklace by Bunny Paige: https://www.bunnypaige.com

Watch by Exquisite Corpse Boutique: http://www.theexcb.com

Sarilda Cowl

It may sound morbid but I spend an awful lot of time in cemeteries, all things considered. For one, I like to play Pokémon Go and they tend to be good places to stock up on in-game supplies, and for another they tend to be calm, quiet peaceful places where I can walk around and think. "Sarilda" is a name that caught my eye on a headstone recently. It's beautiful and quietly elegant, just like this cowl.

Required Skills

Knitting in the round

Lace from charts or stitch pattern words

Simple increases/decreases

Size

One size

Finished Measurements

Length: 9.5 inches / 24 cm

Circumfrence: 32 inches / 81 cm

These measurements are post-blocking. Length is measured from the tips of the points on either side.

Materials

Clara Yarn Shetland 1.0 (100% Shetland wool; 300 yds / 247m per 92g / 3.25 oz skein); color: Moorit; 1 skein

US#4 / 3.5 mm circular needle

Stitch marker

Yarn needle

Gauge

24 sts and 28 rows = 4 inches / 10 cm in stockinette stitch

Pattern Notes

Lots of bang for the buck on this lace pattern that's suited even for absolute beginners. Yarnovers (yo), ssk, k2tog are the only stitches used.

The stitch count of this pattern changes from round to round, but begins and ends with 17 sts per pattern repeat.

Until the pattern is established, it can be helpful to use stitch markers every 17 sts to ensure correct pattern placement.

Stitches and Techniques

Sarilda stitch pattern (beginning and ending with 17 sts)

Rnd 1: Knit. 17 sts

Rnd 2: K2tog, k6, yo, k1, k6, ssk. 17 sts

Rnd 3: K2tog, k13, ssk. 15 sts

Rnd 4: K2tog, k4, [yo, k1] 4 times, k3, ssk. 17 sts

Rnd 5: K2tog, k13, ssk. 15 sts

Rnd 6: K2tog, k2, [yo, k1] 8 times, k1, ssk. 21 sts

Rnd 7: K2tog, k17, ssk. 19 sts

Rnd 8: K2tog, k15, ssk. 17 sts

Rnd 9: Purl.

Rnd 10: Purl.

Pattern

Using your favorite stretchy method, cast on 187 sts. Join to work in the round, being careful not to twist, and placing a marker to denote beginning of rnd.

Rnd 1: Knit.

Rnd 2: Purl.

Rnd 3: Purl.

Work Rnds 1–10 of chart or Sarilda stitch pattern a total of 5 times.

Total stitch counts for each round of stitch pattern:

Rnd 1: 17 sts = 187 sts total.

Rnd 2: 17 sts = 187 sts total.

Rnd 3: 15 sts = 165 sts total.

Rnd 4: 17 sts = 187 sts total.

Rnd 5: 15 sts = 165 sts total.

Rnd 6: 21 sts = 231 sts total.

Rnd 7: 19 sts = 209 sts total.

Rnds 8, 9 and 10: 17 sts = 187 sts total.

Rnd 54: Bind off knitwise.

Finishing

Wet block, and pin the points of the stitch pattern, until thoroughly dry.

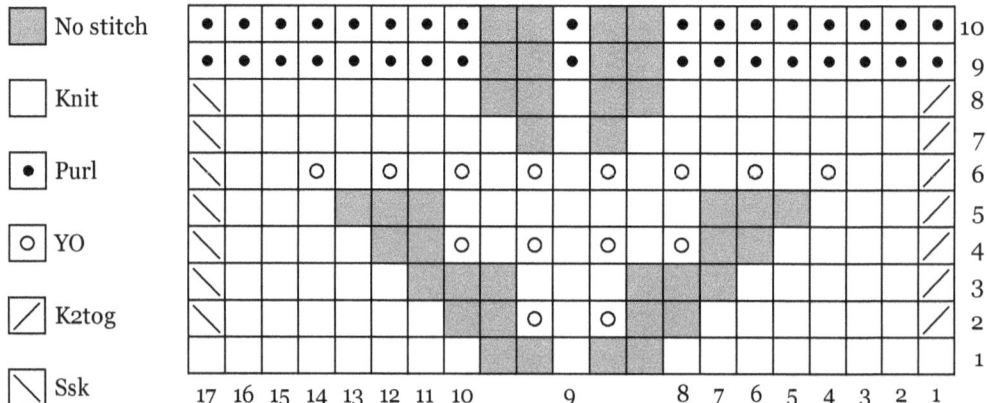

Shadowtime

The Miss Babs Ansel colorway just calls to me with its lights and darks—I love the dimensional look of the fabric it creates. Combined with a highly textured surface like this one where open holes and high/low areas provide additional visual play for shadow and light, you get a fun, fast knit that looks a lot more complex than it is.

Required Skills

Knitting in the round

Following pattern from words or chart

Intermediate increases

Simple decreases

Size

One size

Finished Measurements

Circumfrence: 22 inches / 56 cm

Height: 9 inches / 23 cm

Materials

Miss Babs Yowza (100% Merino; 570 yds per 226g skein); color: Ansel; 1 skein

US#6 / 4mm circular needle

Yarn needle

Gauge

22 sts and 28 rows = 4 inches / 10 cm in stockinette stitch, blocked

Stitches and Techniques

Cowl stitch pattern

The stitch count changes throughout this pattern, however, it will always start and end with 14 sts.

Rnd 1: Ssk, k9, k2tog, k1.

Rnd 2: Ssk, k7, k2tog, k1.

Rnd 3: Ssk, k2, yo 3 times, [k2tog, k1] twice.

Rnd 4: Ssk, k1, M5, k1, k2tog, k1.

Rnd 5: Ssk, k7, k2tog, k1.

Rnd 6: Knit.

Rnd 7: K2, [yo, k1] 6 times.

Rnds 8, 9 & 12: Knit.

Rnds 10 & 11: Purl.

Pattern

Cast on 154 sts, and being careful not to twist, join to work in the round.

Rnds 1 & 2: Knit.

Rnds 3 & 4: Purl.

Rnds 5 & 6: Knit.

Work repeats of the chart until you have about 15 yards left, or your cowl is the desired height, work Rnds 1 - 6 once more. Bind off.

Finishing

Weave in all ends and block to measurements.

- ☐ Knit
- • Purl
- ○ Yo
- ╱ K2tog
- ╲ Ssk
- ⊗ Yo 3 times
- V⁵ M5 - (k, p, k, p, k) into next (yo 3) st

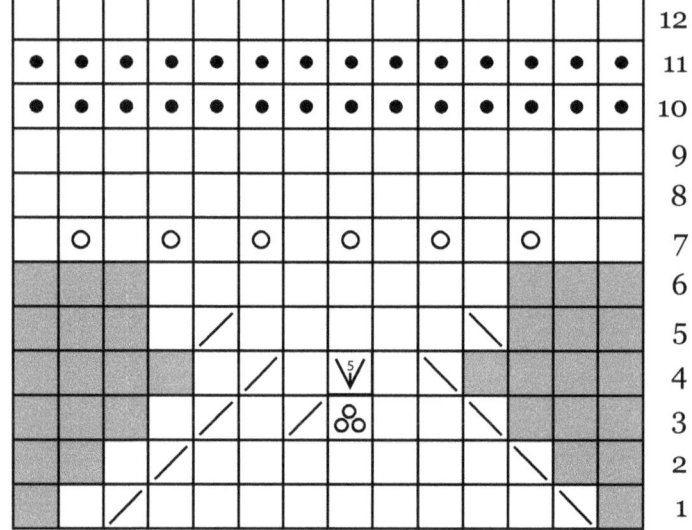

Abbreviations

- **1/1 LC** – place next st on cn, hold in front, k1, k1 from cn
- **1/1 RC** – place next st on cn, hold in back, k1, k1 from cn
- **1/1/1 LpC** – slip 1 st to cn, hold in front, k1tbl, p1, (k1tbl) from cn
- **1/1/1 RpC** – slip 2 sts to cn, hold in back, k1tbl, (p1, k1tbl) from cn
- **2/1 LC** – place next 2 sts on cn, hold in front, k1, k2 from cn
- **2/1 RC** – place next st on cn, hold in back, k2, k1 from cn
- **2/2 LC** – place next 2 sts on cn, hold in front, k2, k2 from cn
- **2/2 RC** – place next 2 sts on cn, hold in back, k2, k2 from cn
- **3/2 LC** – place next 3 sts on cn, hold in front, k2, k3 from cn
- **3/2 LC** – slip 3 sts to cable needle, k2, k3 from cable needle
- **3/2 RC** – place next 2 sts on cn, hold in back, k3, k2 from cn
- **5/5 LC** (left cross): slip 5 sts onto cable needle and hold in front, k5, k5 from cable needle
- **5/5 RC** (right cross): slip 5 sts onto cable needle and hold in back, k5, k5 from cable needle
- **cn** – cable needle
- **k** – knit
- **k1tbl** – knit through back loop
- **k2tog** – knit 2 sts together
- **kfb** – knit into front and back of next st
- **M1L** – use tip of LH needle to lift strand between sts from front to back; knit loop tbl (increase)
- **M1R** – use tip of LH needle to lift strand between sts from back to front; knit through front loop (increase)
- **MB** – make bobble: (k1, p1, k1, p1, k1) into next st, turn, k5, turn, slip 2 sts, k3tog, pass 2 slipped sts over
- **M5** – make 5: (k, p, k, p, k) into next YO3 st.

- **p** – purl
- **p2togtbl** – purl 2 sts together through the back loop
- **pm** – place marker
- **rnd(s)** – round(s)
- **RS** – right side
- **sl1, k2tog, psso** – slip 1 st, k2tog, pass slipped st over – 2 sts decreased
- **sm** – slip marker
- **ssk** – slip as to knit, slip as to purl, knit the 2 slipped sts together
- **st(s)** – stitch(es)
- **W&T** – wrap and turn
- **Wrap 3 st** – [with yarn in back, slip next 3 sts to RH needle, bring yarn to front, slip 3 sts back to LH needle] 3 times, ktbl, p1, ktbl.
- **WS** – wrong side
- **yo** – yarn over
- **yo3** – yarn over three times

Patron thanks

Almost 300 patrons signed on to support #knitgrrl52 on Patreon from its launch and through the first year. Without their financial support and enthusiasm for the project, I could not possibly have taken on something of this size and complexity. I am incredibly grateful for all of my supporters! This list is current as of 15 May 2018—I plan to continue the Patreon in a modified format, so check out patreon.com/knitgrrl to find out what's going on now! Again, my deepest thanks to all of you!

A. Robin Avila
Afton Koontz
Alicia Harder
Aliza Nevarie
Allison King
Amber F. Lee
Amy Duvendack / BadAmy Knits
Amy Lipkowitz
Amy O'Malley
Amy Shelton
Anna Correll
Anne Smith
Annette Wilhelm
Annie Vanaskie Watters
Antje Gillingham
April Ridgeway
Billy Zayac
Bonnie Callahan
Bonnie Groening
Caitlin Bright

Candice Bailey
Cara Henderson
Carole Chesser
Carolina
Carolyn Blakelock
Carolyn Myers
Catherine Dean
CathiBeaStevenson
Ceri Davies
Charles KNITexan
Chelsea Loo
Cheryl Monroe
Cherylann Schmidt
Chloe Sparkle
Chris Lynch
Christine Jones
Christine Tubbs
Christine Widgren
Conchi Rodes
Crystal Hanson

Dana Kashubeck
Danielle Taylor
Deborah Jackson Weiss
Debra Husby
Debrielle Welch
Dee Minturn
Deenna Dains
Deirdre McNeill
Denise Pratt
Diane Nishri
Dianne Shantz
Dindy Yokel
Donna Hulka
Dorce Campbell
Dragonfly Fibers
Duranee Dodson
Eileen Gruber
Eliza Sheppard
Elizabeth Green
Elizabeth Stromme

Elizabeth Theresa
Ellen Boucher
Erin Mullins
Erin Wolff
Esther Bozak
Faith Love
firstfallen
Fran Bee
Frances McCarthy
Gail E. Maddox
Gaye Houchin-Copeland
Gayle Clow
Glenna Eastwood
Glori Medina
Hanna Hintikka
Hazel Daguiar
Heather Ordover
Heather Risher
Irene Speir
Ivete Tecedor
Jacquilynne Schlesier
Jamie Wang
Jan Arnow
Jan Campagne
Janet Clark
Janice Stenger
Janine Le Cras
Jean Belman-Herrera
Jean Link
Jeanne Tufano
Jeff Pinto
Jenn Ridley
Jenn Wisbeck
Jennifer DeAlmeida

Jennifer Hovis
Jennifer Lindberg
Jennifer Wollesen
Jenny Dicastri
Jenny Schoohs
Jerre Dawson
Jessica Steele
Jessica Stowell
Jillana Holt-Reuter
Joan Grahlfs
Johanna Bowline
Julia Johnson-Roy
Julia Kerbl
Julia Knitterlythings
Julie Aronson
Julie Lindsey
Karen Boykin
Karen Fazioli
Kate Brehe
Kate Graham
Kathryn Beyers
Kathy Beaumont
Katie Hughes
Kelsey Leib
Keri McIntyre
Kim Burkhardt
Kim Fuller
Kimberlee Gillis-Bridges
Kitty Hamersma
Knitty Magazine / Amy Singer
Kristin Hansen
LA Bourgeois
Laura Gilman

Laura, Ben & the 4 Dog Crew
Laurel Luchsinger
Laurie Johnson
Laurie Starr
Lea Vollmer
Lee Bernstein
Leni McCormick
Lesley Robinson
Leslie Behm
Linda Hawkins
Linda Randall
Linda Schiffer
Linda Sutherland
Linda Walker
Lise McKinney
Liz Gipson
Lora Felts
Lorraine Dolsen
Louisa
Lynn
Lynne Wolters
Magda Stryk Therrien
Margie Smith
Marie Amer-Westmeyer
Marie Bryan
Marie Duquette
Marion Gibson
Marion Regeste
Marsha Auguste
Marta Poling
Mary Dagnan Wills
Maureen Foulds
Meg Helmes

Melissa Gaul	Psuke Bariah	Sue Roth
Melissa Hellman	Rachel Clark	Susan Burgerman
Melissa Taylor	Ray Janikowski	Susan Jones
Merlene	Raymonda Schwartz	Susan Miller
Merry Rubins	Rebecca Armstrong	Susan Wilson
Merryl Rosenthal	Relaxing With Yarn	Sylvia McFadden
Meryl Dorey	Robin Stewart	Sytske Corver
Michelle Heckman	Rosemary Moore	Tammy Moorse
Michelle K	Sabrina Pauch	Tan A Summers
Michelle Kennedy	Sam B.	Teresa Dannemiller
Michelle Toich	Sandra Fleming	Teresa Emery
Monika Stramaglia	Sandra Zetterlund	Terri
Nan	Sandy Kolher	Terri Emery
Natalia Forrest	Sara Beckwith	Terri J. Rau
Natalia Uribe Wilson	Sarah Devantier	Tuulia Salmela
Niki Curtis	Shannon Coon	Ulla Martin
Nyriis	Shelley Harper	Under MeOxter
Pam Daley	Shelley Kinder	Vicki Lynch
Pamela Schultz	Shelly Minton	Virginia R Jones
PariserLandluft	Stacey Melquist	Yael Weiss
Pat Fisher	Stacy Person	ZhanTao Yang
Paula Wilson	Stephanie Mcguckin	

About CP

Cooperative Press was founded in 2007 by Shannon Okey, the author of this book and many others. She had been doing freelance acquisitions work, introducing authors with projects she believed in to editors at various publishers. And although working with traditional publishers can be very rewarding, there are some books that fly under their radar. They're too avant-garde, or the marketing department doesn't know how to sell them, or they don't think they'll sell 50,000 copies in a year.

5,000 or 50,000. Does the book matter to that 5,000? Then it should be published.

In 2009, Cooperative Press (cooperativepress. com) changed its name to reflect the relationships we have developed with authors working on books. We work together to put out the best quality books we can and share in the proceeds accordingly.

Thank you for supporting independent publishers and authors.

Cooperative Press can be found on

- Facebook: http://www.facebook.com/cooperativepress
- Instagram: http://www.instagram.com/cooperativepress
- Ravelry: http://www.ravelry.com/people/cooperativepress
- Web/shop: http://cooperativepress.com

  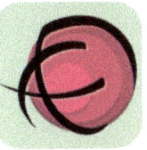

www.ingramcontent.com/pod-product-compliance
Lightning Source LLC
Chambersburg PA
CBHW042135160426
43199CB00022B/2919